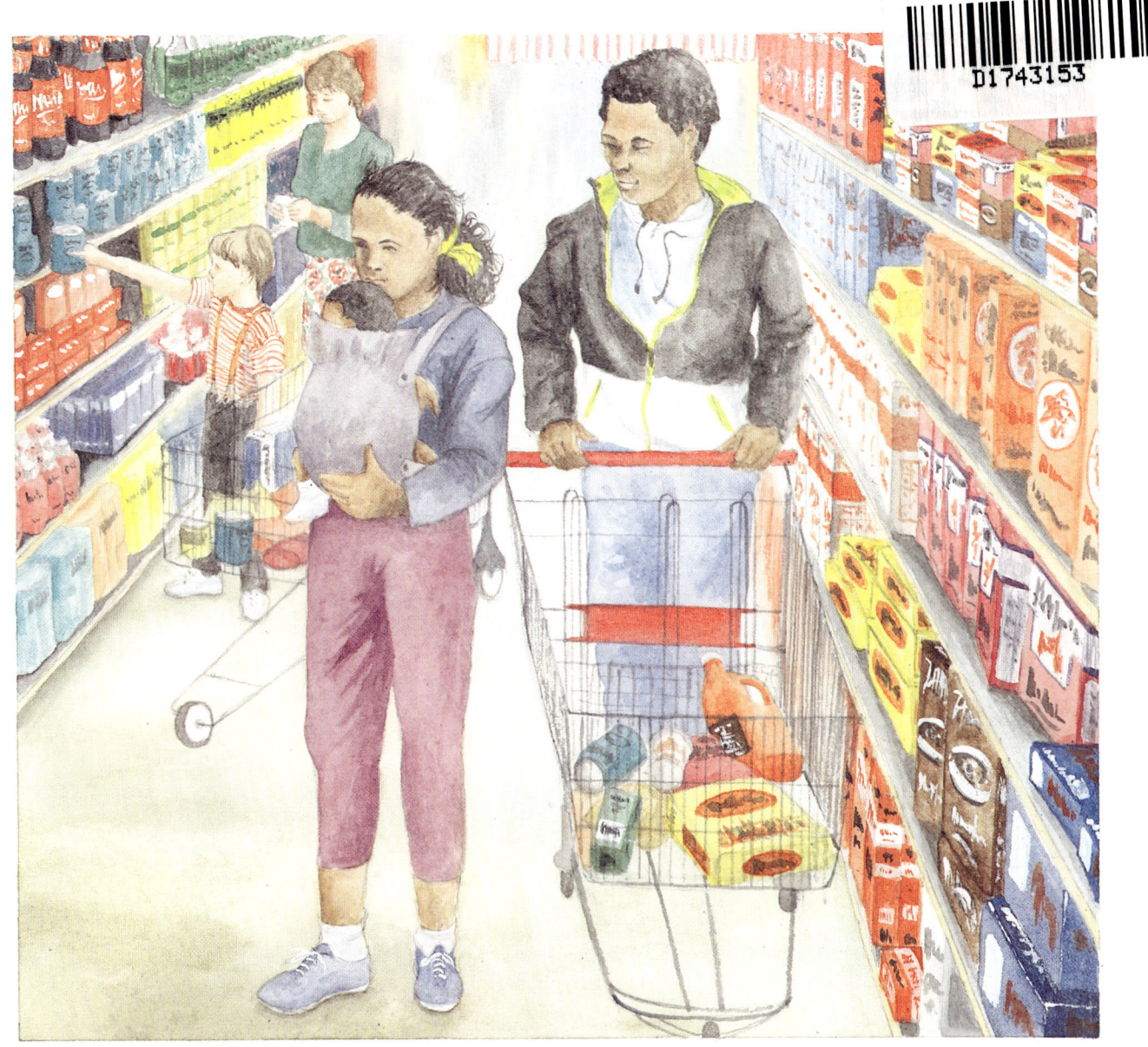

We're a family.
What are we doing here?

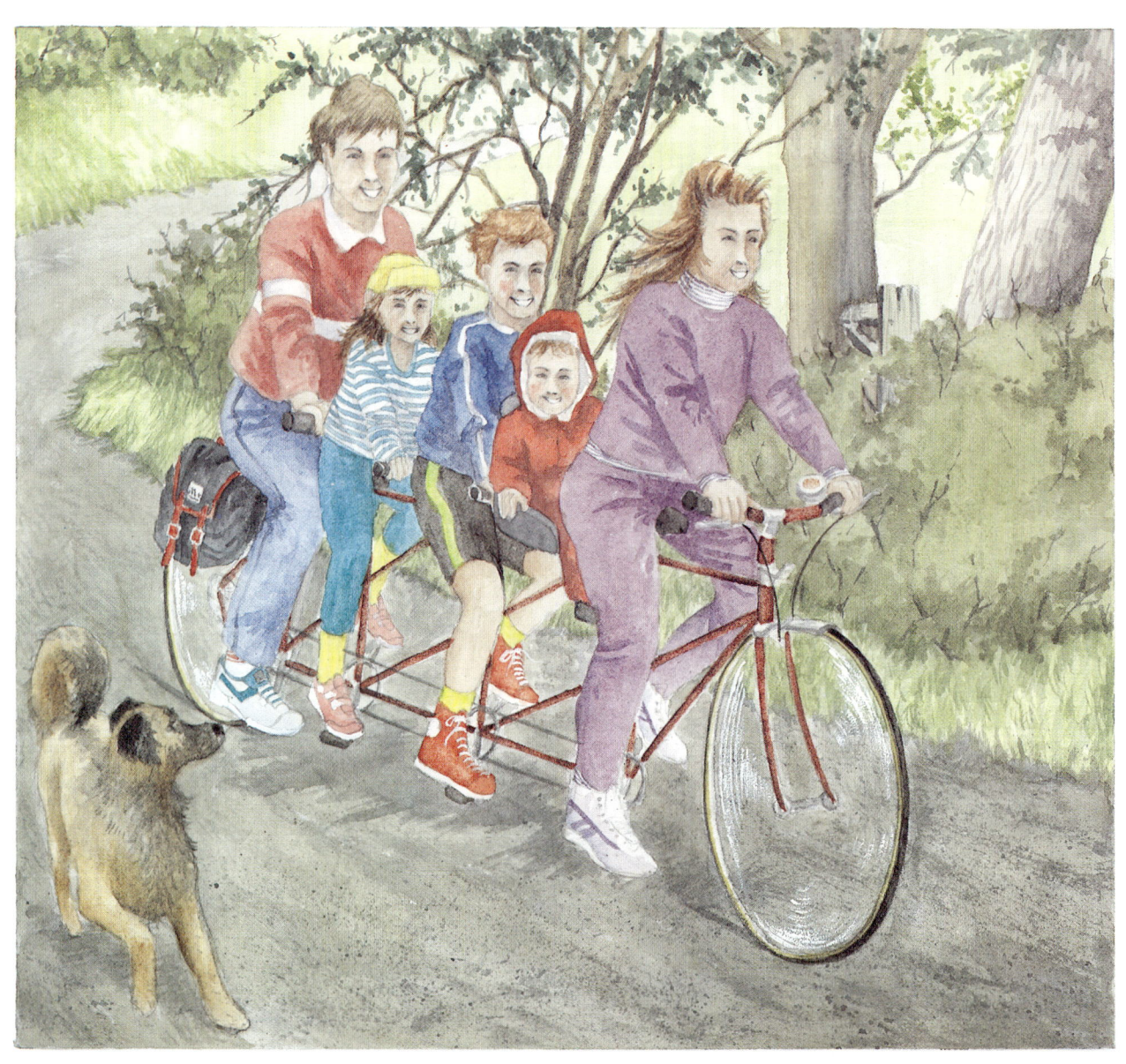

We are a family.
Where are we going?

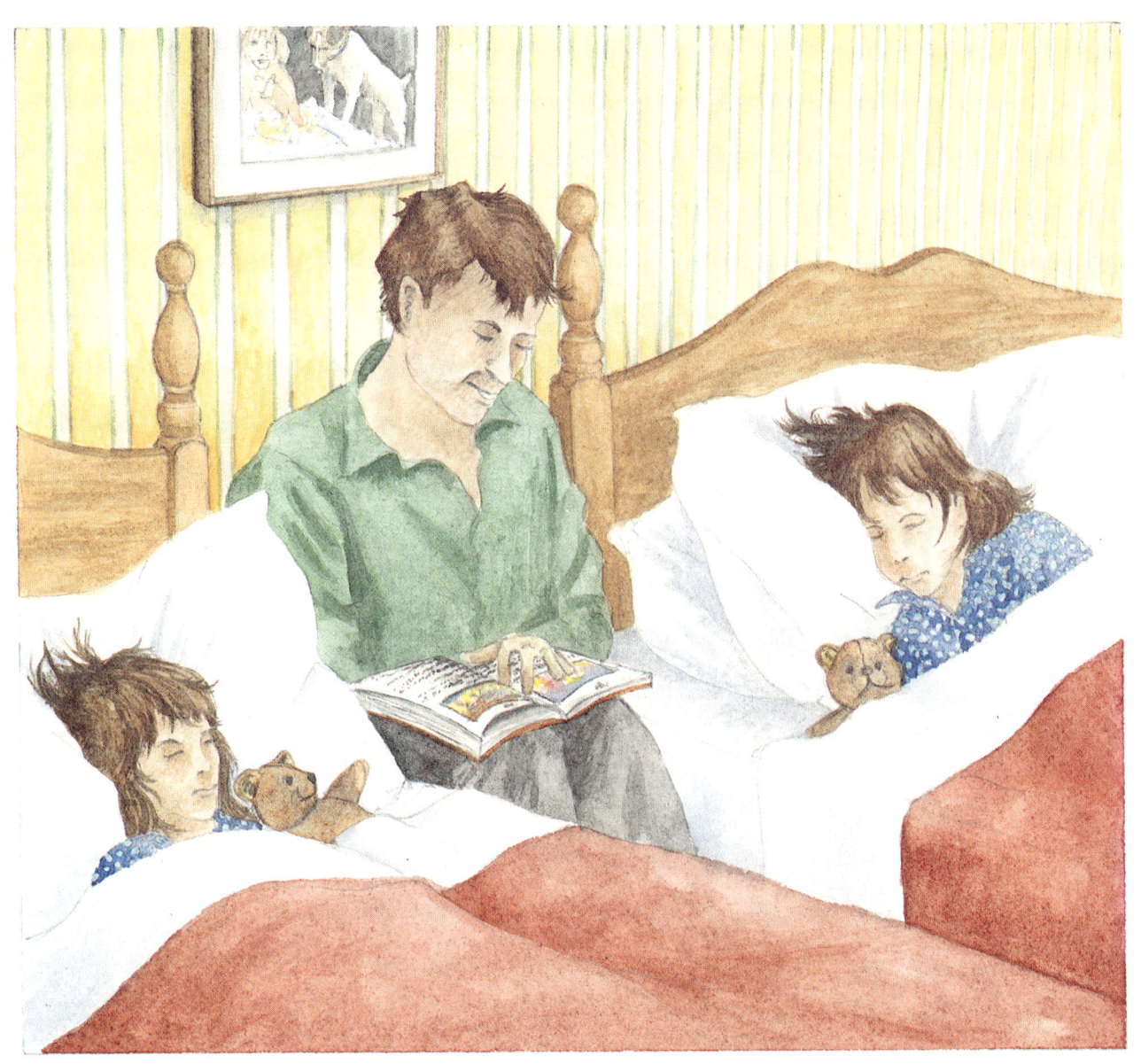

We are a family.
What are we doing here?

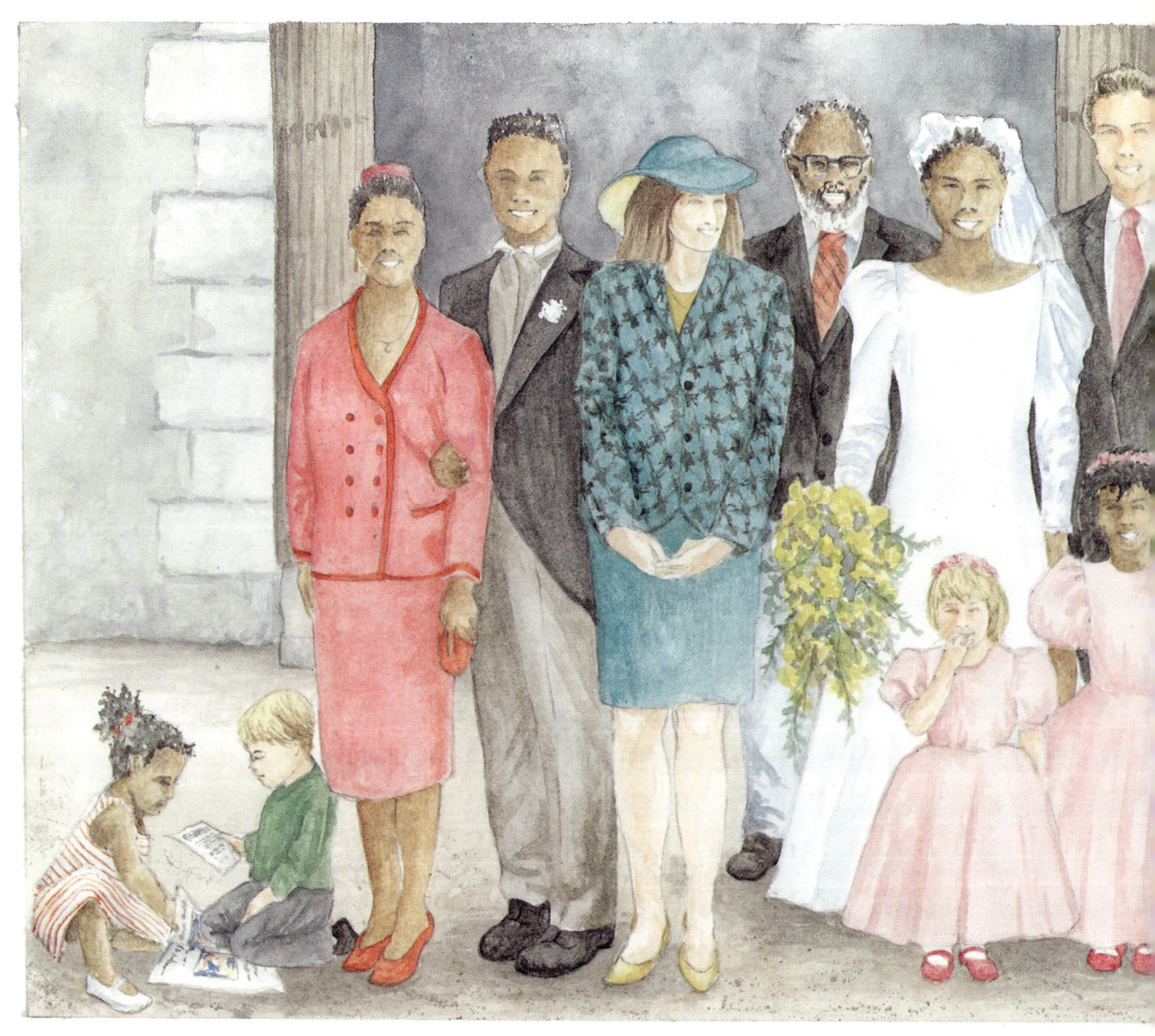

We're one big happy family.

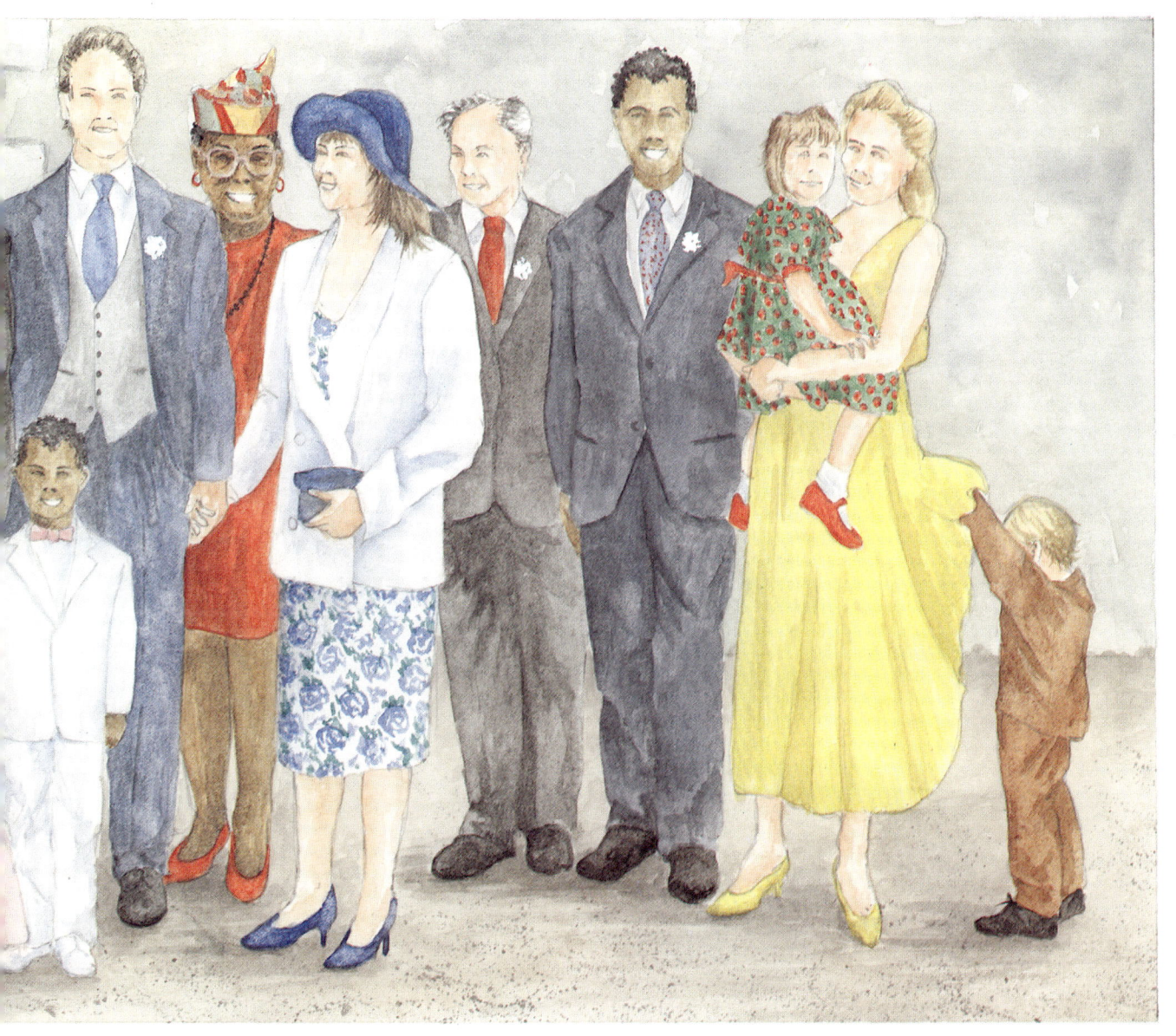

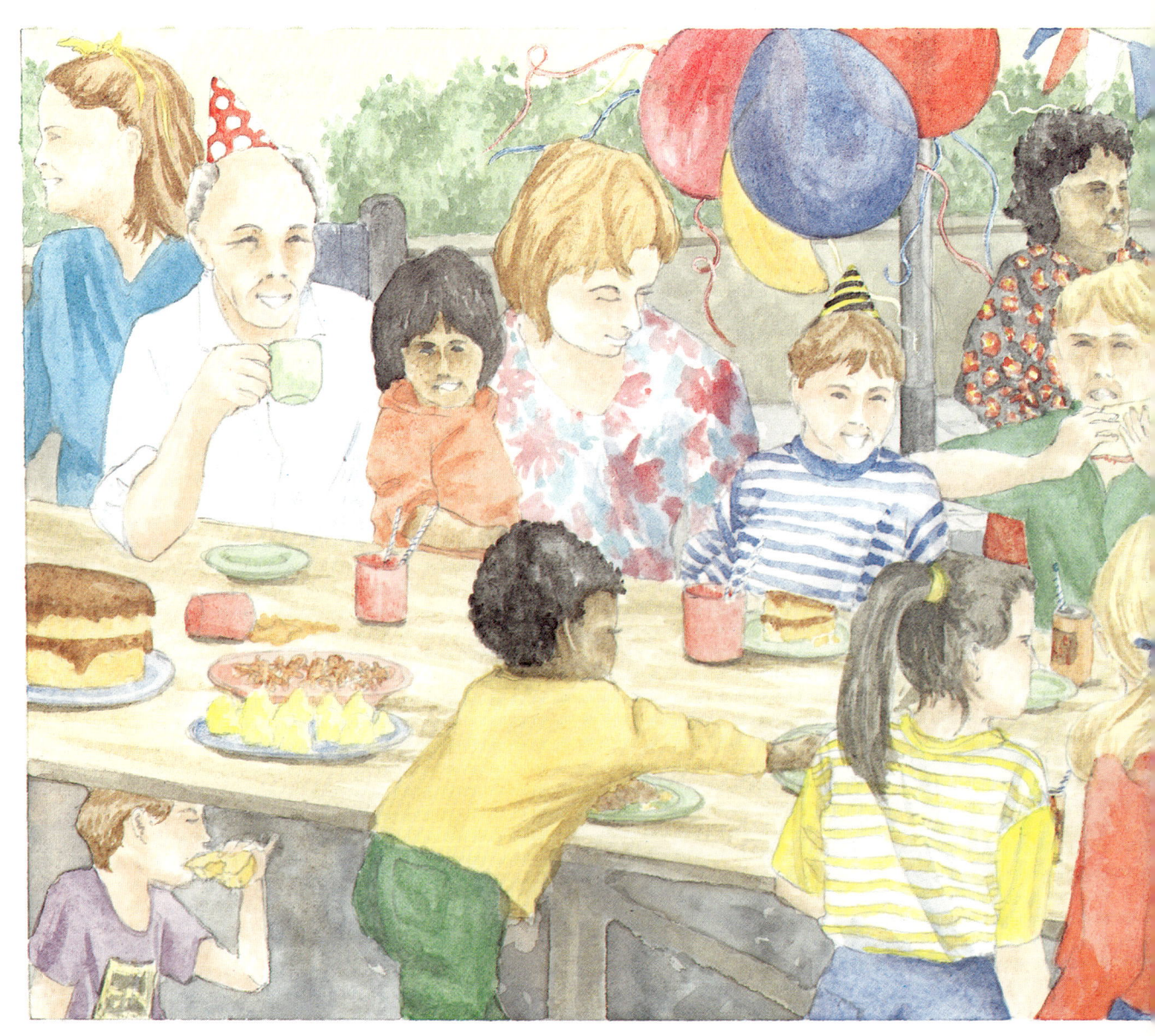

We're like one big family.

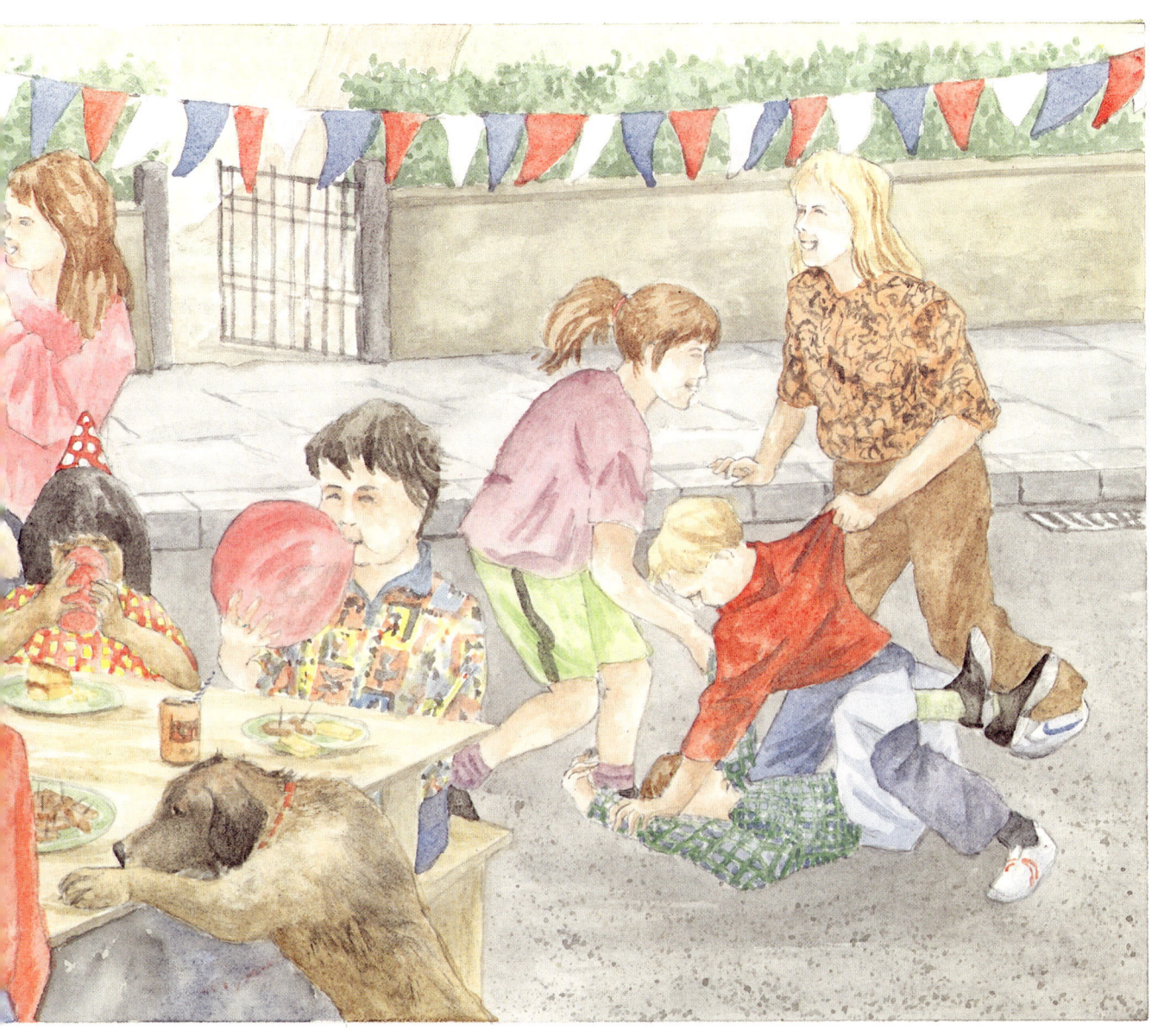

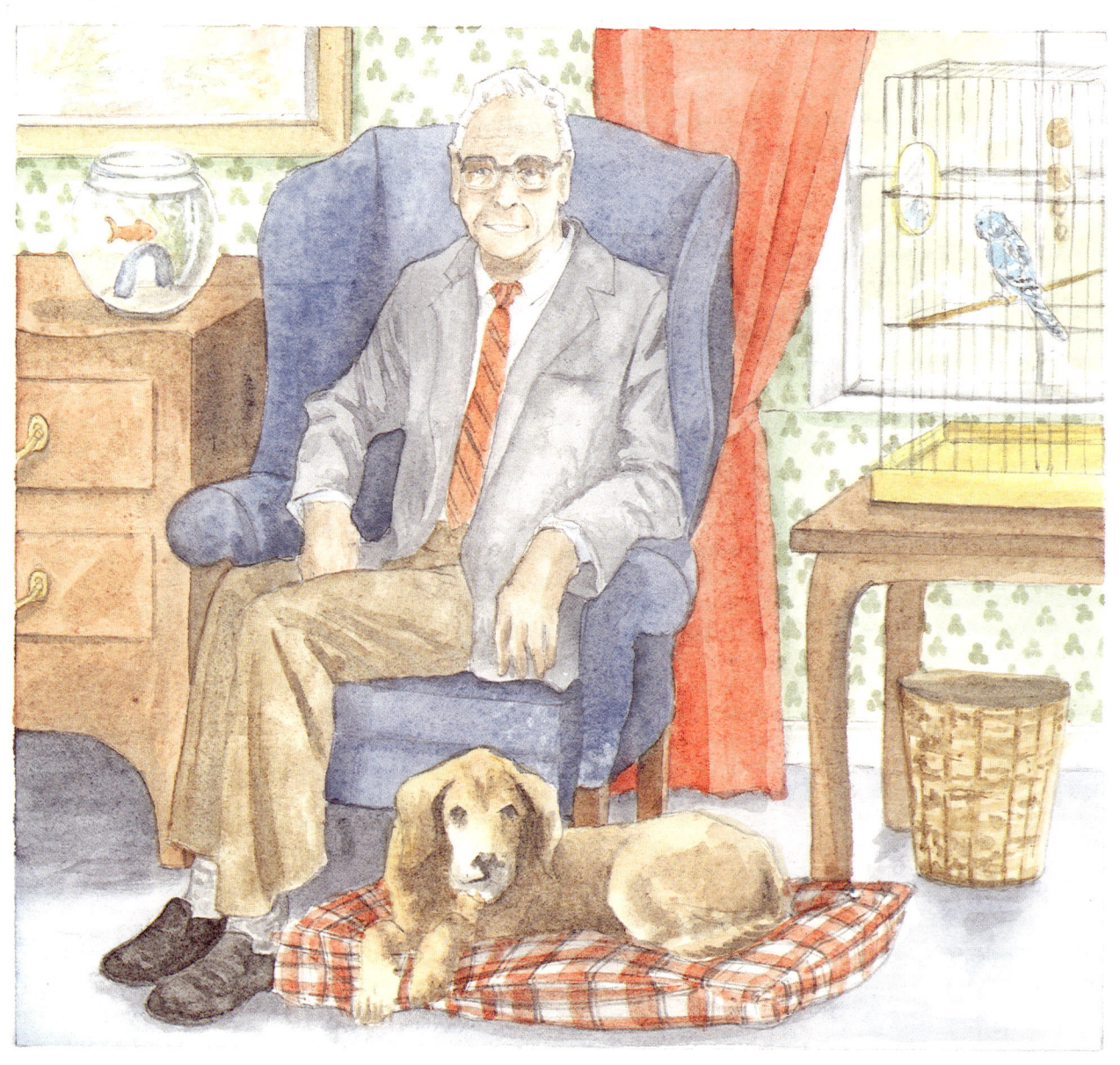

This is my happy family.